THROUGH
THE TREES
OF
AUTUMN

Other Books By Janet Krauss

Borrowed Scenery

The Unpinned Eye

THROUGH
THE TREES
OF
AUTUMN

POEMS BY
JANET KRAUSS

SPARTINA PRESS

Library of Congress Control Number 2007900752

ISBN 978-0-9791735-0-9

Printed in the U.S.A. by
Morris Publishing
3212 East Highway 30
Kearney, NE 68847
1-800-650-7888

For my parents, Simon and Leah(Lena) Hentoff

Simon, who gave me his need for camaraderie, his buoyant spirit and dignity of self

Leah, for her love of dance, sensitive soul and teaching me the art of writing

To both of them for their unfailing love

Acknowledgments:

Some of these poems have been published in AMARANTH, CALIFORNIA QUARTERLY, ROCKHURST REVIEW and WEDNESDAYS AT CURLY'S.

My love to my family: Bert, David, Simon, Bonnie, Cheryl, Rachel, Amy, Anna, Ben and Nat who have been sources of sustenance and inspiration

My gratitude to my many good friends who have supported and encouraged me in my poetry

My special gratitude to the Faculty Development Fund Committee of St. Basil College for their financial help in the production of my book, and for their warm appreciation of my work

Contents

Prologue

Coda

Prologue

"The purpose of poetry is not to persuade
but to explore."
  Chase Twichell

"A Cage Went in Search of a Bird"
Franz Kafka

It is rare my bird flies from her cage
though the door is always open.
I have to find her and bring her back
to sing a new theme. I hope she recalls
the words so I can hear them, see
them tumble slowly into place.

They need to lead me to their place.
Then my bird will return to her cage.
I will be centered in the present, see
past all loss of words, my vision open
in the now with no need to recall,
sense the emptiness once in back

of me, no draft behind my back,
instead form and content in place
and relief to luxuriously recall
what to feed my bird in her cage--
scenes of autumn or windows open
to spring over the scent of the sea.

Or a glimpse of two by the sea,
one's hand on the other's back,
talking in a low voice, openly,
grateful for the solace of this place.
Or a study of a panther in his cage
and wonder what he recalls.

Or the sight of swans that recall
possibilities my bird will foresee
while she waits in her cage.
She must be patient, not flutter back
and forth and leave her place.
I watch for nuances, blinds to reopen

so I can revisit old scenes to open
new ideas my bird will recall
and nurture as seeds to grow in place:
to watch a child at play and see
him forlorn later looking back
when just curiosity lived in a cage.

I will rinse my bird's eyes to see
to bring new thoughts back
or recall in place, her opened cage.

Poems

1 Howland Street

It stands, three stories tall,
ruddier than seventy years ago.
It stands, a statement,
to me alone, "I am still here,
I stand for you."
Its bricks, red like Jacob's pottage.
But the birthright is mine.
No deceitful exchange.
I walk up the few steps,
the stoop on the right chipped
now, the stoop where
my mother ordered me to sit
to get well in the sun,
the stoop where the neighbors
tched, tched when I brought
Ruth to visit, Ruth
of a darker skin;
the stoop where the trolley car
conductor tried to lure me
away on his day off; the stoop
where I saw a man play
with himself in his car
across the street.

I walk up the steps
and peer through the glass door.
It is dark inside, but not for me
to put away childish things,
but for me to clearly see
where I lived on the right,
where my mother shook
the knob over and over
to make sure the door was locked,
her mouth, a thin, determined line
of vengeance, a litany of curses
unfolding in her mind.

The hallway floor and the stairs gleam,
polishing my childhood, making it
shine in its root like a firm bulb.
My childhood--my brother sighting
the men in the white coats coming
to take me away
because I sucked my thumb.
My childhood--playing hopscotch
in blue chalked squares,
finding my balance
under the awning of twilight.

As I walk away I turn to face
the window --my bedroom.
Now a nondescript bowl and cup
sit on the sill. No mother looking
out, calling me in for supper,
or looking for something
far beyond the line of trees,
looking for something not possible.
I view the window on my left--
Martha's room where her mother
one afternoon put her to bed,
naked under the sheets,
the dark green shade drawn,
the shade used for air raid warnings.
Put to bed because of the thrill
of the steal--toy soldiers
from the 5&10.
My mother sent me outside
free after her words of wisdom.
I loved her for that.
Martha's window sill was and still is bare.

And there was the same mailbox
on the corner of Howland and Warren
where my father sent off business letters
at a certain time in the evening,
with a look of anxious purpose in his eyes.
And on that corner I made up stories
and then ran into the house to tell
my parents, and they believed me.

The Swan Boat Ride

He was only three
when I arrived
in a black suit and rode
the swan boat with him,
his hair curling softly,
his eyes dreaming
over the watery path.
With the quick joy
a child owns
he smiled at the ducks
following as they do now.
I am the same age
as my parents were
when they died.
I had returned
for the unveiling.
I did not cry, not then,
strong in the dignity
of grief. Forty years
later only the boat
is on slow time,
as I meditate among
the willows and grasses,
the curves and bends
of the tranquil route.
In prayerful silence
I pay tribute to that day
and to my small son,
steering me safely on.

On the Porch

My eyes travel through the bars
    to see my father
resting after a heart attack
    forty-five years ago, waiting
in the shade on another porch,
    waiting for us to come back,
    as he yearns to be
where we are, yearns to
    side stroke the water
as it assents to his glide,
    shredding his worries,
churning them into scintilla
    moving in with the tide.
But the heart's fear grounds
    him and feeds him a nugget
of despair while his desire
    pulls like the call of whales
lengthening miles of ocean.
    He cannot pretend
as the bearded New England
    writer did that the field
outside his window was the sea,
    and Greylock Mountain, a whale.
He cannot be a part of
    such silent intimacy.

At the King Solomon Memorial Cemetery
   for my father

In a dream your younger grandson met you sitting
against your gravestone, taking a break, enjoying
the night air and the slight breeze, a smile of leisure
(so seldom seen) on your face as you chewed a weed,
your white, wavy hair under a wide brimmed straw hat.
You wore overalls, your hands in the pockets.
So you had wished to be, a farmer like your father.
So your namesake envisioned, a dream within a dream--
a vision that tries to erase my sight of you, staring out
the window as you sat in your living room chair, staring out
into the free air you no longer could explore, bound by
the fraying of your heart. But your grandson released you.

Of course you were not there when your older grandson
came to visit having found in his way to be near you
in the sense of this place, this plot well cared for
as he was pleased to see, in the sense of his story
linked to you he knew only through pictures, when
you held him and fed him at three weeks old,
his thin, tubular arms resting by his sides,
eyes closed as his whole tiny being drew in
the sustenance of his life. You marveled at that.
He left on your grey, granite stone a World Series
Red Sox Champion cap. He left on your grey,
granite stone his love for the Red Sox too.

I hope the wind does not blow it away.
I hope it will fall to rest on the bed of your earth.

A Walk and a Coffee

He wanted to be alone
with us. He wanted to walk
while his family napped.
A sentience passed between us
to last beyond the unhurried hour,
an awareness natural
as that between flowers
and summer air or the flow
of river beside a bank of trees.
We neared a row of vintage
buildings in the process
of renewal, the blank windows
exciting promise in their spaces.
A fountain spilled its splendor.
With the self-assurance
of something rich hidden
within him, he said, "You knew
I would like to see all this."
And under the shade of the elm
across the street, we savored
the coffee as his inner thoughts
began to surface,
but it was time to go.
We looked behind at the fountain
in its robust overflow,
his words stored beneath.

The Tree House

The father built a tree house
guaranteed to expand with
the width of the tree,
guaranteed to expand with
the plans of the children
when they set sail in search
of sea monsters, or take
solo flight inside books
where women are knights
and owl-glassed boys
fight the wicked of the world,
and when each child
can plot private thoughts
lying on the wooden floor,
looking up while motes
spiral in the boundless air
as the years rise
and dissolve in the skies.

The Lost Child
   for John

I walk the beach
watch the water
fold itself
undo itself
mutter and run.

A baby steps from the foam.
Molluscan buttocks and belly,
hair the color of bleached weeds.
He tips forward and raises his arm.

The air retreats.
He wears the command of fathers
as he stands upright
secure on his bottle shaped legs.

I have to bend to hold his fat starfish hand.
He signals for me to close my eyes.

Space expands as we enter the water.
Secrets breathe invisible as clams.

As I walk the ocean floor,
my breath forms sharp hills.

In no time we cross a zone,
a sand bar, sure under foot.
The currents run only one way
and calmly accompany me
while light like the one left
on over night to calm a child
flows by my lids.

When a sense of place
rises about me,
its steady breath of warmth,
he taps my knee.
I open my eyes,
and stand on another shore.
It flatly shines
like the moon by day

while a colony of babies,
the color of conches
toddle about,
their bodies wet with
the skin of water.
They pat the tidal pools awake,
divide shells in the pearling mud,
and fill holes. No day escapes.

A milky light keeps watch
and enters my body, sure of its intent.
I quietly break forth,
and join the communal counting of shells,
touch vibrating hands in the passing.

No night binds the stars.
We sleep at intervals
on this edge between.
I feel I have given birth
to lambs as the lacteal air
nourishes us and my mind glistens
bare as their skins.

When my time is over,
they raise their hands
and hundreds of starfish wave.
I have to go back alone.

A wildness sucks my breath,
leaps in my ears, swells my eyes.

My head is an ocean.
I hurtle over the sand bar
and float in a trough.

The waves spew me out.
My feet slap the mud
and my breath returns
the length of the shore.

Milky whispers from a distance
brush my shoulders.
I cup my hands over my ears
to hear.

The diurnal sun heals
and I watch the water
fold itself
undo itself
mutter and run.

.A Certain Time of Year

It allows for the couple, fairly new
at being old, to shed their coats
and look at each other
at arm's length as they hold hands,
walking towards home,
laughing at some jest
known only to them, cut free
from the cord of their history
to float for the moment.

It allows for someone to climb steps
and unlock the front door
as if he were the prodigal son returning,
the warm air stirring him
to renew vows, forget
the journey rigid with winter's weight.

It allows for a leisure at twilight
when the sun is in no rush to leave,
so its amiable light visits a room,
favors the carpet like a cat finding
its place. It extends a chance
to be a part of the intimacy,
the colors deepening,
richer than clustered jewels
as dusk's shoulders draw close.

The Romance of the Stone

Someone said the stone is a revealer
of time, a soothing acceptance of what
cannot be grasped: the spin of years,
a silent echo in an empty well
and lost-- the lamb fleeing from
my hands or a chance to talk
to one who rounds a corner
with quick, muffled steps.

I watch a rock write its own future
in glyphs of cracks and lines, and think
of Gilgamesh setting his story
eternally in stone as his organic self.
And the niches of crumbling ruins
shove grass upward to show
the world the thrust of life.
Birds soon quietly nest therein.

Only a Glint
for Elizabeth Bishop

The words wash down the river,
minnows schooling off,
towed by the skein of the sun,
not the big fish the poet caught,
whiskers, barnacles, staring eyes
and all. She finally let it go--
the poet's victory.
My small fish leave me only a glint,
a sparkling.
If I put my hand into the current,
they will scatter faster,
lose their shine.
Better just keep them lit in my mind.

It's That Jewel of a Pause

It's that jewel of a pause
we crave and treasure:
pen in hand, poised in
mid air before the blank
paper, before the first
stroke or word
anticipates the page.
It's the hummingbird
before it whirs toward
the center of a flower;
the haughty heron
at the moment
he is twinned
in the pool
beneath him.

And it's the eyes
that open
at some revelation
but close again
fast before further
inroads are made
as if night eclipsed
morning
forbidding the unfolding
of the natural day.

The First Stage

In the depth of winter fish swim
  beneath a lid of ice
wearing that orange-gold glitter
  that threads the lightest of saris,
and the minute globules clinging to their fins,
  a nascent stage between water and pearl.
They are patient tadpoles of shimmer,
  waiting for you to put your ear
close to the ice. Listen first to their woosh
  bumping into your cheek, falling back,
until they are ready to whisper
  heartbeats for poems.

Rain

The girl on the Morton's salt shaker box
strides along under an umbrella
as a shower's bold strokes fall
behind her. "When it rains, it pours"
is the message over her head,
not the dire warning
that frogs of trouble will descend,
but the guarantee nothing
will impede the flow of the salt
of our lives, running free and clear,
while words like fingers of water reach
toward and salt our wounds:
keep them cleansed of infection,
and soothe like the earth-scented warmth
of the first spring rain, that follows
the girl under her wide umbrella
on the Morton's salt shaker box.

As You Walk
For Maxine and Don

Listen to the water,
a light pummel of clarity
over the rounded rocks--
he is there.

When the wind and rain provoke
the curdle of waves to ride
in with your muted anger,
he is there.

When a swan whitely startles
as if from nowhere,
a measure of grace glides close--
he is there.

Let him raise you above
the morass into the new,
sharp currents of air–
he is there.

The Delay

It is late October and the trees are tight
in their green, fooling themselves
that they can stay unchanged
in the mild-scented wind soon to
announce its own colors. I want to see
the leaves break fast and eat the air
with the zest of their brilliance.
I will walk through the orchards
of orange, plum and apple hues,
miniature mirrors playing with the light.
And I will be the one holding on
like a child to her mother's dress,
not wanting to let go, fearing a place
where limbs shiver, crackling
in ice that can neither glitter or yield.

Sleep
   after the painting by Pierre Puvis de Chavaness

These are mythical people
whose muscular arms bear
the imprint of hard honest work.
Here, by the water,
on the receptive grass,
they set aside
their iron pots, hoes, ploughs,
and lie down--
the men, women, children--
lie down and let sleep
fill the vessels of their drained bodies.
Some huddle together.
Others sprawl.
A mother sits against a tree,
her draped arm,
a cradle for her baby.

The light of the moon,
as it awakes at the edge
of the horizon,
as it rises to watch
over this race,
cools their bare backs
and tracks the water
like the rungs of a ladder,
Jacob's, no longer in use:
these people need not see
angels running up and down,
wings and feet flashing
on the liquid steps.
These people sleep
without dreams,
blessing their own ground.

No heat or wind or cold
visits them,
only the wash of the moon.

Rachel, a 19th Century Naturalist
   (eighteen months old)

You keep company with those
who tracked the fields and woods
over a hundred years ago:
you observe and linger long

as they did over stones and moss.
Like the poet of Amherst
you carefully trace
a butterfly on its course.

You stop to bend over tulips.
"Flower," you dub each one
and ceremoniously cup
them with your palm.

From a bridge you watch
water streaming past rocks
and listen with the ear
of the man who heard ice

crack on Walden pond
at the end of winter.
And you track the path
of the smallest ant

with the same precise eye
that guided the hand
to tilt Peter Rabbit's head
or hunch his rump.

As a test you drop
an acorn into the loam
dark hollow of a tree stump,
stir, study and rescue

the nut, faithful to the find
of your day. You march on,
your face reflecting the light
of the limitless sky.

The Messenger
for Amy

She likes to appear unexpectedly
behind the one with white hair
    dancing to the right
    and to the left of her

as she stands by the window,
eyes lost amid the interplay
    of light and wind
    over the water.

Or the harbinger leaps
from a corner or springs
    up before her and always
    she startles, and each time

she laughs a scattering of chimes.
Such is the response to the angel
    without wings. Such is
    the dialogue of their love.

Our Pictures
For Anna

With the softest of white wool
I'm tying together the pictures
of your life I'm pleased to own:
you sitting at the ocean's edge
hearing a secret in the waves
to share with your family
waiting at home,
you standing outside in the night
listening to the moon's secret
and she, yours–the silent bond
between the two of you
as she looks you full in the face;
my drawing the ladies
of the Emperor's court,
as you hover over me, watching
the lotus blossoms appear
in the black pouf of hair
and the wide billows of sleeves,
slender lily petal hands beneath.

And when you were little
the pictures of how we made up
stories about Tikka
when she gathered shells and straw
for her grandmother
and wove baskets with her
as you weave love and stories
with me.

Prophecy for Ben
  (5 months old)

Your father said you watched the fireworks
with interest but without concern
for the sound as if it were distant enough
not to be heard. You stared, unblinking.
You watched with eyes that contain
the changing colors of the ocean,
the ocean that keeps in holding for you
this glitter that now takes command
of the dark, this glitter which will appear
as a glint as you smile when you awaken
to the masters of the universe
who will drench you with the golden skirl
of music, Euclidean hoops of dimension
and hieroglyphic clues to the scintilla
of life you will find in a silent pond
or an ivy covered house with someone
taking shape by your side.

Rachel in Denmark

She pocketed the scenes
in the purse of her heart
to preserve how the buildings
were strung throughout
the organic-woven streets,
how the sky was inviting
as she walked the cobblestone
pathways, past statues and fountains,
how the sky was inviting,
more room to take in
the strollers arm in arm,
the lovers holding hands,
the children chasing each other
and vendors selling cinnamon rolls.

Eighteen years ago
she crawled to the tree
on her lawn, stood up
and looked past
the bower of leaves
where the sky was inviting
and caught, limitless,
in her eyes.

.

Depending on Light

On the most overcast of days
  it skims the water
    or remains a steady sheen.
A serenity one tries to assume,
  the clouds kind in summer,
      patient in winter.

On clear mornings
  it provides a just washed view
    unaffected by the burden of heat
or gloom that may interfere
      as the hours progress
        until the evening.

Then it folds itself up
  like a bolt of cloth making room
    for the shadows that move
in, tenants draping themselves
  over night, but at dawn they pull
    back, depending on it,

an agreement they have,
  silent as it is,
      and wished for by those
who find not even a mute communion
  exists between them and others,
    no unseen, palpable glimmer.

Reflections on Tour

There is no breath under the worn carpet
loose underfoot like the skin an aged cat
wears as he prowls alone in the dark.
Chandeliers hang high over ghost-lit seats,
exhausted, faithful retainers
while Greek gods wanly kneel
along rows of balcony tiers.
The fallen ceiling fills the stage--
collapsed, black leviathan--
where once flashing legs
and rising voices leapt across the floor.

Someone long ago stuffed a rag
now stiff with grime in the missing
pane of a glass door--a gesture
of care before the draft of ruin
seeped through the haven of dreams.
A gesture of care like a touch
on a shoulder or an intimate whisper
that deafens the footsteps of fear.

Something Was Not Right

The rain does not fall
in its usual, soothing way
against the window
as I work at the desk.
The rain slashes the side
of the house
like an angry elephant tamer
obsessed with his power
whipping the hide
of the beast
who just stands there
waiting with patience
large as his size and weight
for the thrashing
to cease.

The morning grows prickly
against my skin
not the engaging, incremental
shift of light
measuring my arm
as noon approaches.

The phone rings–
its sound blocking
the blows of the rain.
I pick up the receiver.
A familiar voice rays through–
and outside a bird calls
and a car slushes down the street.

A return of temporary semblance
as when a pair of ducks
mated for life
appears from a cove
and coasts along the shore
as if out for a Sunday stroll
until the sky glowers,
and they disappear.

I'll Be Home This Evening

She answered the phone and said,
"I'll be home this evening."
Something of quiet drama and comfort
to hear her say this, ready to
pick up the receiver when shadows
of trees brush against the windows.
She'll engage in conversation,
give and take advice
while scenes of past years visit
the embrace of upholstered chairs,
children's voices close to their lessons,
radio voices selling Lux soap
in between scenes of suspense
that could not possibly compare
to every day lives where
the mole-like mundane dwelled.

After the phone call,
she'll sit beneath the compass
of the lamp light sparking her white hair,
book in lap. She'll turn on the TV
for the 10 o'clock news,
then take a walk, a slow one,
from room to room so as not to disturb
the memories too new to collect
dust on the mirrors, the uncluttered top
of his bureau, his desk.

She would welcome a little mystery,
the kind that when it arrived
would nest in her hand.

Walking With the Waves

Why this exhilarating murky agitation knocking
the buoys off their perches to struggle in the water
as you arrive at low tide, leaving behind miles of seaweed
and tiny snails on the flat, wet, dependable surface?
The seaweed fringes the widening shore like extended shawls
of fishermen's wives. The snails, imperceptibly rolling beads,
begin to settle. Merciful clouds extend a mild, comfortable
morning, and I yield to the expanse of light and shore while
I think of the couple Halcyon and Ceyx who, in their love
for each other, willed themselves into birds that always roost
upon your crests. Such is my elan so firm, I welcome
the susurrous remnant of a storm you bring from some unseen
region, and thrill to that as part of my belonging here
at this juncture before habits change with the new season.

The Seder

We take our time on this night.
We ask more than the prescribed four questions
as we lean on the white tablecloth.
We ask, in particular, why we eat potatoes and eggs
dipped in salt water.
Potatoes--stubborn growths making their way out of
dry, stony earth.
Eggs--so perfect in shape
we want to hold them at arm's length for praiseworthy view.
Sources of life anointed with a wash of salt
as from our fear and sorrow.

So we nod our heads to the contraries of life:
the first, fierce yelp
and the last, guttural escape.
Or the brief, simple relief like an ocean breeze
on a boardwalk, the water and lighthouse clear
in our view, then suddenly made desolate
by a change in the weather,
bringing the fleet of doubts back to the harbor.

We take turns around the table
reading the story of Exodus, resting on our cushions,
the custom to honor our freedom,
but what will comfort us when we are numb to chills,
when we confront the bondage of our unknown fates?

We open the door to Elijah.
His cup of wine awaits him.
On the draft of air we feel his presence,
hear his robe brush his sandaled feet.
We want to believe the wine in his goblet diminishes,
his sanction of a flawless lifetime
for all of us about to pass from hand to hand
a heaping platter of steaming food.
We take our time on this night.

I wish to be

Noguchi's fountain,
its water emerging
from a constant
source rising unseen
as if eyes were shut,
thoughts on one focus:
to form the flawless,
liquid cloth across
the surface of the stone
and to fall, fully draping
its sides, unceasing,
sure of its calm.
Drops of rain do not disturb
but silver point their way
and join the stillness
of the flowing, join in
the ongoingness
as if life could go on
like this forever
with imperceptible erosion,
and one's purpose,
never stopped, shining
in its triumph,
grounded by support,
as dependable as basalt.

Moonlight Creature
   (after a print)

Strange, little creature,
neither seal nor penguin,
lit by a crescent moon
hazed in either a mystical
or atmospheric phase,
five stars as escorts,
you stare at me. You want
to say something: admonish
or advise. Are you suggesting,
through your black eyes,
what someone wrote,
"It has always been.
Just as it will always be,"
or are you trying to show
me by example
to accept time and space
without boundaries?
With deference
and decorum
the Japanese wave
and wave goodbye
to someone until
he is out of sight.
I cannot do so
because you are never
far from my view
even if I am not standing
in front of you.

On White

It covers an egret like poured cream
into the water of his reflection,
and attracts the eye when a swan
decides to lift across the pond.
We stop raking to look up
unlike Bruegel's plowman
when the blanched legs of Icarus fell.
He did not know about unusual
disasters or wonders, this man
who depended on the earth
to succor him. He did not have
the luxury to cast his eye to net
or to miss dreams in the air.

It creates the unicorn, his soft mane
rising as he gallops our way.
If we wish, he will lead us into woods
where we cannot get lost, where hosts
of trees part as he lowers his head.
If we wish, he will purify the water
with his horn, the farther out we wade.

On Space

when you enclose
the missing within
your mind,
attentive to words
that outdistance
the calls of birds
answering each other

when the length
of a room
along a wall
sweeps the eye
clean and you watch
elan leap across
the bare floor

when old men
sit close on a bench
and talk about sports
or news of the day,
crushing the void
they left behind
in sunless places

In the Japanese Garden

Here the mind is swept empty
of all thoughts raked away
by light furrows in the sand,
dissolved by the smoothness
of the round stones covering
the bottom of the pond
and those guiding your steps
past miniature waterfalls
and shallow streams.
A stone pagoda lantern
greets you, steadies your eye
along the path onto the bend
of a bridge and near the whisper
of a low, bamboo fence.
Hedges bowed like monks
usher you into the gazebo.
There you can imagine
gold globules of rain
singing off its tile roof.
Then listen to the silence before
the hush of the chimes answers
the slight summer breeze, know
they do not toll time.

Cold

The distance a wizard withdraws into,
pale and drawn in the narrow doorway
of his remaining years in a magic store
in Denver. Thin ice seems to cover
the cornea of his eyes, sightless
to those who pass him by
seeking, on a whim, the wares of his trade
glittering on the shelves of his store--
tales of enchantment and sleight
of hand, magic lanterns and secret codes.
"Magic is a craft," he mutters under
the small blizzard of his beard rough
as worn rope. No one listens.
His robe gleams the ages of gems
and frayed velvet. No one notices.
No one notices the tall mannequin
in the narrow doorway of his
remaining years.

He Chose to Wait for Her

He chose to wait for her,
their eyes askance, avoiding
the weightless swell of want
they both felt pressing close,
yet far.

Was it best not to have talked,
best to have thought kind words
lay mute, hidden like a moon
holding half itself
in its round shadow?

There was a stillness between them,
not that of a mild, windless time
when benign snow falls through
interstices of silence.
But he chose to wait for her.

On Blue

Helen Keller's eyes shone blue like the water
glanced at dawn, a blue borne for a short while,
from a place only some people know, like
Helen who thanked a poet for teaching her
to hear lily-bells and find where black-eyed
susans watched her, and ferns brushed her knees.

When Pinocchio knocked on the fairy's door
she wore an evening blue that matched
her hair, a blue that rescues all of us from
dangers, forgives our misdeeds and restores
us to Gepetto, peering from his window
every day or waiting at the end of his street.

Alice's gown was a floating blue that swept
her across the room and unto the other side
of the door. After the dance was over,
and the white-gloved servants disappeared,
she sat withdrawn into instant memory,
her shoes off, the gown, limp around her legs.

In Whistler's painting his twilight blue rolls
easily towards us over the water, lulls us
like the moments as we drift into sleep.
The masted ships follow, taking their time
to anchor in home port, long before
the wind stirs and the sky checks out.

The Arrival, 1914
after the painting by C.R.W. NEVINSON

The transatlantic ship reached
port, its bow triumphant
in scope defying the emergent
mythic water god of long ago.
From the stacks smoke drifts
off in skeins more graceful
than Aphrodite's hair
as she rose from her shell.

Figures on the projected deck
below face the sea, remain
still part of their ocean journey.
They are not ready to turn
and face the strictures of the hard,
paved roads or what brought
them here. There is no sign
of war in their sight.
Is the outbreak what they fear?

The slight, stationary men
do not know they are fixed
in place for us to contemplate,
for us to accurately predict
the past as it churns relentlessly
ahead for the next nine decades
into the encroaching mist.

January, 2003

I take home a souvenir from the museum shop,
a picture of a ship, a man-of-war at sea.
And I think of our troops massing off to the Middle East,
all neatly pressed into their fatigues.
How delicately the ship is drawn, its fine lined rigging
and the civility of the waves below
like that of the two elderly women on the train
addressing each other, cocooned in fur coats,
self-assured in the steep of their years.
And I think of the young woman at the exhibit,
striking in her red scarf, as she exchanged
sharp retorts with her escort. And I think of comfortable
older couples gazing past bucolic landscapes.
All these I think about as the pert-eyed girl
across from me, flanked by luggage, asks aloud
if she's on the right train because she's on her way home.

On Green

The trees in summer are excessive
adding more depth and height
each year like layers of dust
that cannot be sorted, a life's
file of works buried in drawers,
labels licked away by time.
The green constricts as one breathes.

It was alright for Baucis and Philemon
to grow into oak and linden leaves
nodding to each other in the heat.
They have a different perspective.
And in winter they patiently wait
in their branches for the first green,
the fluid color of sea glass lit by the sun.

This is what the swimmer views
as she makes her way through the water,
thankful for its brief passage for relief.

A Street Scene

They swirl about each other
in the honey light of their youth,
these girls, their smiles flying,
hair whiskbrooming the air.
They do not know, not now,
not at this mellifluous moment,
that around the corner
someone's walking away
from someone else
without a passing word,
without calling out
or rushing up
to fall in step.
They do not know, not now
of such goings-on,
so much a carousel
of each other they are,
their chatter and laughter
the melody of the ride,
these girls, brazen
as sun caught in a mirror
barring the approach of shadows.

The Present

It's what we live for
so we can save
some of its glitter--
only the status of shine--
turn its many facets
in the hands
of our thoughts
like the way a moonstone
catches the blue of sky
in the right position of light,
or the way
the long-fingered hand
of a dancer skims
his partner's face
for a twist of fire to stir,
or the way
a synapse sparks eye to eye
or the way
two can walk
in synchronous rhythm
as their ideas ignite
like apostolic flames
atop their heads.

It's what we live for
before the rude
or gentle footfall
that crushes the last
of what glimmers.

Uncle Rudi
Germany, WWII
after the painting by Gerhard Richter

He poses for you
as anyone
would before a journey
or moving away.

With a soft stroke
you brush wet paint
quickly across
his portrait
so you can see time
blur this moment
distilled here
as your uncle stands
at ease, comfortable
in his new, long
double-breasted uniform.

With a soft stroke
you reveal
his compliant smile:
he appears unaware.
He appears
without guile.

The Vigil

We tried to protect the candles
   with a wall of cardboard
to block the wind,
   the candles lined up--
like children standing close
   together before the doors
open on the first day of school;
   like the needy waiting
in a soup kitchen,
   for the warmth of kindness;
like flowers struggling,
   flickers of upturned collars;
like soldiers, knees
   trembling before an attack,
1,000 breaths soon quenched
   like the flames we cannot protect.

After Winter Landscape with Skaters and a Town Beyond, 1788
by Johannes Willen Tingeler

We are granted a glimpse from the past--
a small scape of thatched homes
fast in the greyness of fog,
windmills and a town in the distance
of our mind's scope and lost
in the motes of more than 300 years.
But near to us a young man pulls
his girl across the ice,
her arms raised in mock protest.
A woman falls, her arms also raised
as if calling to the geese
in the flying clouds.
A boy kneels to tie his skate
as he watches a dog barking
at a man looking up at the sky.
All this going on, this flurry
of living confirmed
on a winter pond long ago,
while always a rowboat waits
for the thaw. And a broken one
half submerged in ice
bears the weight of time.

It Is the Time of Year

It is the time of year
  when summer heat exhausts
itself and retreats
  to the side of the porch
where autumn coolness
  collects in the shade
and allows for a respite
  of calmest calm
to take me unawares
  like windless tide
the night-filled sand.

It is the time of year
  to visit the water's edge
and turn my pockets
  inside out and let the lint
and stale crumbs,
  troubled thoughts, drift
off into the ocean's depth,
  along with the bent clips
that have grown tired
  of holding onto papers
no longer in my hands,
  no longer dependent on me.

It is the time of year
  to find the russet scented breeze
after the deluge of rain,
  find the right amount of sunlight
to equal the first comfort of shade,
  line my pockets
with shiny clips to keep together
  the new voices
that travel with me
  as I walk into the bright wind
with a smile of thanksgiving.

On Measures of Time

Lingering sun
  in corners of porches--
    autumn warmth
      at end of day
        hoarding
          unhurried time

Empyrean stillness--
  powdered medallions fall
    in a spell,   spaces apart,
      the sound of rush
        in some other place
        and distant time

The first leaves,
  turning the air
    with small hands
      soon buried
        in summer's
          thicket of time

Leaking heart valve--
  a frenzy of gulping noises.
    What do they thirst after?
    I call to them,
      "Please slow down,
        please take your time"

Travel with Them

Angels follow the sun someone said.
Travel with them, they are careful,
their wings never melt
like Icarus's. No plummeting
into despair but they can lament
death wringing their hands in the air.
Keep a steady pace
so the breeze will stay cool–
ablutions of well-being.
Pass with them over thresholds
sparing children's lives,
watch them carry armfuls of souls
to bliss and hear Horatio wave
them on as they accompany
Hamlet to his rest. Hold on
to the stream of their song.

Plucking Poems
April 2006

One picked "Loveliest of Trees"
on the loveliest of days
in early spring
as I sat before the class
sprawled on the slight rise
of earth as some popped
handfuls of sod
down another's back
or flicked twigs
at each other's sleeves
all at the same time extolling
 the boughs budding
around us, or the frogs
in a poem, frogs that brave
the new world in a hop
across a dark road
or announce warmth
filling tentative air.

One picked "The Great Farm"
hearing again the bees,
and seeing wings of birds
scape the sky
and knowing how the farmer
large of size sets his buckets
down beside the cow.

One picked "The World Is Too Much with Us,"
the plea to listen to the winds before
they close for the night
and watch the moon expose
the furrows of the ocean.

Another picked "The Lake Isle of Innisfree"
for the lull of sounds where violet
appears at noon and the evening
flutters in with a message of peace.

I picked "The Grapefields as a Child"
when the poet ate "from the clouds
that tug at the ground," his dreams
that need release, that need to fill
a house full of plenty.

The works alluded to in the poem were by the following poets
respectively: A. E. Houseman, Norman MacCaig, Philip Booth,
William Wordsworth, William Butler Yeats and Benjamin Durango.

As if We Were Schoolgirls
   for Sheila

As if we were schoolgirls,
we walked up the stairs
together to the classrooms,
glasses of water in hand
as we drank in each other's words--
concern for the students,
concern for each other,
ideas about movies,
how one differed
from the novel which revealed
much more than the film.
So in life we pondered why
some reasons were concealed.

As if we were schoolgirls,
we left notes in each other's mailboxes,
your ever present Harpo signature
so like you, a warmth and humor
you have blessed me with:
how you opened the curtains
in the faculty dining room
because closed, you said
in that comedic tone of yours,
the place looked like a funeral home.

When luck fled from you,
humor left for just a short while,
so courage and strength
could fill its hole.
And yet the curtains
had to be opened
for you are a child of light
and love and we will always
walk up the stairs together.

The Awakening

The baby stares at her hands:
Fish flex their lives before
her eyes, hearts pump
back and forth or
fronds waver under water.
Wriggling starfish rise
phosphorescent from the sea.
Or night stars come down
to gaze at the child
transfixed by her autonomy.

Then she glances
at the backs of her hands--
bad luck she senses
as if she heard
ancient Chinese whispers.
The palms hold
the blind mirrors of her future.

An American vista
flaps boldly before her,
fosters her choices,
this child,
whose tiny hands
had lain quiescent
bound by mute ignorance.

Now they flutter
like bold butterflies
around the mouths
and eyes of new love.

The Cameo
for Marsha

Our friendship
is like the cameo:
the fresh-faced girl
finely detailed atop
the sepia colored shell
our youth integral
to our old age
firmly set together
as our timeless caring
for each other.

Whispering Sibyls
  for Gladys

We are always walking under the bower of trees
in full leaf across Franklin Field
finding the right place
to wrap our dirndl skirts around our legs
and hug our knees, the cumulus clouds passing
by, as we talk about our wishes
and our husbands-to-be-
"He's quite handsome"; "How lucky you are!"

We were our own sibyls
sculpted in the kindest of breezes,
sculpted in our trust in each other.

Through the Trees of Autumn

Trees still green, fully leafed,
conduct the even-tempered winds,
and direct my walk
through shift in light
and air that lifts my step
past sheltered homes
to the turn on Main
where a men's shop stands
that makes me stop,
and gaze back in time.

I dimly see my father,
the salesman of long ago,
in the doorway
of the narrow structure
that houses stacks of sweaters,
shirts, pajamas,
pants, rows of suits--
a display of plenty
and order layered
with the odor of months
of storage.

I see him enter,
pause with hand
in coat pocket
as he gathers the lint of hope,
clears his throat
and greets the owner
with a dry grip
but winning smile

as strong as this light
on the now empty threshold,
as strong as this light
that barely brings
my father into focus
as strong as this light
that honors him.

Grove Hall

Its name sends up shadows
that murmur and bend
around the neighborhood.
Its name is the drugstore
in the middle of the square.
A vanilla scent ushers us in
as if from a frosted well.
Beyond the door it is safely dim
like arms waiting for me.
Ceiling fans gently hum
and lull the air.
Jack is always there.
When I hoist myself up
the veined marble counter
is a shock of cold to my bare arms.
Black and white double scoop, please.
I retreat near the comic book rack,
nurse my ice cream
and keep an eye on the two figures
cast in the sun: My father leans
over the counter to talk to Jack.
My father's hair and skin
are as white as the marble.
Jack's hair gleams black
as the tiles on his floor.
Eyeglasses glint in the light
from the morning window.
I take my time finding the right
Donald Duck, and float through
the bright painted day of the comic book.
I listen to my father and Jack
mingling voices, catch a word
as if on a wave that carries me to shore.

I watch my father laugh
and I see hills sway in the distance.
He hunches his shoulders,
his back, a shining plain.
I do not hear him
laugh at home.

On Yellow

Nights, the ceiling light deepens
the yellow walls of my mother's kitchen.
She's at the sink, washing the supper
dishes with a zeal I always admire--
so easy to do and say, "Task well done,"
though she never expresses such words,
while I worry over my homework...

Passover Eves, the setting sun is the color
of the yellow checkered tablecloth,
the matzoh, matzoh ball soup,
matzoh meal muffins, this yellow
resting on my father's Haggadah
as he gently chants through the story.

Years, the yellow of my kitchen
hums with the voices of my sons
as they eat their cereal, macaroni
with cheese, tease each other
or keep secrets to themselves
while I am compelled to recite
the day's pageant of trauma
or lecture on my studies while
the boys feign a collapse
and my husband laughs and listens.

One day, the walls are primed
for someone else. It is time to leave.

A Daughter's Open Account

I peer through crib bars
hearing your approach.
You are coming closer and I smell
the dust of travel on your business suit
and I fear the sex of you.
There is a stranger's smile on your face.
Do you have raincoats in your black sample cases?
Did you bring me anything? I do not remember.
Memory is the shade under trees now.

When I am five we stroll hand in hand to the drugstore.
You swing me over cracks in the sidewalk, never miss one.
Chocolate soda for me as you chat,
"How's business?" "Did you hear about...."?
Sometimes Arlene comes too, your niece I hate
because she looks like you because she isn't like me
because you smile at her and swing her with the other arm,
shadows blocking a hopscotch square.

On Sunday afternoons you take Ma and me for a ride.
No talk, sullen faces. Empty streets.
Why doesn't Ma look at the dogwoods?
She glares into her sky of sorrows.
You and I wish to be,
the brick of yearning heavy in our chests,
wish to be with Al and Rebecca, Estelle and Anne,
but Ma isn't talking to her sister for seven years.
The monotony of the journey ends.
At Howard Johnson's, the castle on the hill,
you lean against the car, eat your vanilla cone,
a little satisfaction in that.
Vanilla belongs to you each time
I smell its arctic freshness.
A bite of yours tastes better than mine.
Returning home, I lean over the car seat
to hear with you, "Who knows what evil lurks..."

And the draft from the inner sanctum hisses around
me and the sun leaves a whisper of what might have been
as I nibble the remains of my cone.
The castle recedes in the distance.
The grail dissolves in my mouth.
Grains of evening fall without mica or quartz.
One Sunday afternoon a year I accompany you
to the salesman's convention
to watch you feel good
to enjoy attention because I am Cy's daughter.
Grand Peddler's Day and you are the most well-liked.
School Street sun on the hotel desk
while I draw, while you take orders and shake hands.
Light pales. Time to go home. Echoes of
"This is what is going to sell this spring, Joe,
a more casual look," follow me down the hall,
into the elevator, out onto the narrow street,
all the years after your voice goes out in the night.

Sunday afternoon visits at the hospital
after your first heart attack–on the bed,
after your second heart attack–on the couch.
A fireman comes to give you oxygen the second time.
It is easier for me the second time.
Moans of angina pain are less.
I see you sitting on the edge of the bed.
Ma rides with you in the ambulance. I feel safe.
"How can you do your homework"?
Mrs. Hyman the neighbor evil-eyed me.
I turn to the oven where my supper
is warming and open my Latin book.
Sunday afternoon visits at the hospital–
you kibbitz with the men on the floor,
hold your own convention. That smile.
You are in control of yourself again
in your striped silk robe, well-dressed
even here and the sun steps ahead of you.

On Friday nights I watch the fights with you.
You place a nitroglycerin pill under your tongue
sit tense at the edge of your seat
but I know you will be alright.
I sit on the hassock next to your chair.
We discuss boxers' strategies,
Sugar Ray's dance, Louis's heroics,
Johansson's hard rights.
Your face the ghost of the tv screen.

Passover: you whisk through the Haggadah
in a pastel chant by the light of the evening.
I am young in my mother's kitchen
and all is yellow at Passover,
the yellow and white checkered tablecloth,
matzoh ball soup, matzoh meal muffins.
It is special for me
to say the four questions for you.
You wear our tradition as a lightweight shawl.
We are only three at our seder.
I wish for my aunts and cousins
to face me around the kitchen table,
but Ma isn't talking to her sister for seven years.
Dinner ends. Dark guillotines.

High Holy Days and I sit beside you in shul.
You do not have to turn your head
any longer to see if I am coming.
I am still young enough to sit among the men.
I do not have to join the women upstairs.
Your hands are at peace here,
your dovecote each autumn
as you show me the place
in the white prayer book,
Baruch Atoh Adonai Eloheinu....

Later in the afternoon you give me a nickel
to ride the streetcar.
Negative rules of the holy days
hold no order for you.
Sunlight all day.

Years later when I am first married
you take me aside and give me twenty dollars.
Imprint of love. "Buy something nice for yourself."
No need to give me money to be generous.
I am not on commission.
Steady open account between you and me

Memory is the shade under trees now,
shadows blocking a hopscotch square.
Grains of evening fall without mica or quartz
after your voice goes out in the night.
Here the sun steps ahead of you.
Your face is the ghost of the tv screen
when the dark guillotines.
But there is sunlight all day,
a steady open account between you and me

The Rose Poem

When Emily offered
  a rose to a guest
  instead of words,
the silence of her gratitude
  encompassed them
  for an instant
that held fast,
  defied the rushing past
  of days that fade
like photographs
  borne on mirrored glass.

When Simon arrived
  one June morning
  the rose bush
outside the window
  revealed its petals
  one by one,
in celebration
  and so I watch
  the roses appear
each year, sometimes
  scant, sometimes
  profuse depending
on changes
  in all kinds of weather.

When my father died,
  I pictured his pale arm
  stretched out to me
like a white rose
  the same gift
  a father gave
his daughter from
  a forbidden garden
  in a tale told to children.

Mine ventured
  into the same place
  never to return.
But I keep the vision
  of the tall-stemmed
  flower and breathe
its fragile fragrance.

When my brother met
  the street singer
  who wooed our mother
through the window of a radio,
  he offered
  with a flourish of his hand
a paper rose in honor
  of their secret romance
  when he waited for her
under the imaginary lamplight
  every evening.

When my mother sat
  in the rose garden
  in Franklin Park,
she crocheted away
  her wrinkles
  and dropped her worries
with each stitch
  as the flowers crept
  close around her.

Anna Akhmatova's Apartment #44
   The Fountain House
   July, 2006

I climb the same stone stairs
pitted with her grief and fear.
I hear her footsteps.
I look out the small window
near the door, the window
as look-out to see
if the Nazis are coming
or the KGB. I feel the weight
of the waiting for the bell
to wrench the air.
Then I walk the long, solemn
corridor where baskets line
the shelves, canvas chairs
and a sled hang on the wall,
all holding on,
brittle glimpses of stilled lives.

In the room facing the park,
the guide quickly steps forth
offering her service with eager
pauses of breath in welcome words
of English as if plucked from bushes.
She names the poets and artists,
the friends of Anna, the friends
preserved in photos around her mirror,
on a brick wall and behind glass.
I point and she gestures
as she speaks, her hands and arms
like the reflections of the bare
branches outside in the courtyard.

The branches, her hands, swaying,
mourning the dead but her voice
pealing bells as she gives
each an identity.

I silently read their fates:
homeless, exiled, imprisoned,
shot, destitute, suicide.
I read one night Anna's son Lev
made dinner for her and a visitor.
Her son, whose face she would soon
see scored by prison bars.

I glance at her white fringed shawl,
draped over an upholstered chair,
spectral in the mirror
enshrined by the sentry of her friends.

A March day

           slips past

as silently as it came

           on its grey boat of water,

the bare trees unchanging

           in the fixed design

of their outlook.

           The mild air leaves

with the night

           just as the saint

who healed an old man

           glides away,

his smile firm,

           as he holds up a hand

refusing payment.

I Concentrate on Sunsets

I concentrate on sunsets
these days in early winter--
the silver blue into gold water
or the steady, still, grey light.
I linger as long as they do
before dark, without mercy,
leaves no trace. So the gatherings
of warm friendships become
a mirror's flash, and finely etched
as in glass the memory
of my pillared high school
and its sequestered courtyard
where we kneesocked girls
crossed from one hallowed
hall to another. Now only
a portion of the neglected brick
wall is left, windows cracked
and ledges cluttered.
A remnant left at least
bristling in the heat or cold.
So I watch the last of the sun
setting in the water, the red
vying with the trees blackening
into a bastion of hills.

Family Thanksgiving, 2000

I
They bring the colors indoors
as November sheds its season's
hues. They bear gifts of the earth:
the sister places spiced squash
on the table; another, savory turnips,
the brother, apple pie; the father,
creamed onions; the mother, turkey
roasted the shade of russet marshes.
The family has grown like pumpkins
on strong, intertwining vines.

II
No longer does the younger
granddaughter, her hair
a nimbus of golden fuzz,
come into the kitchen
to remind me of the dishes
still in the oven. Now her hair
is slicked back in a bun
and she talks of swim meets
and races won. No longer
does the older granddaughter
take me aside to sing
a Thanksgiving song
about a sleigh ride
to Grandma's home,
a child's wonder
in her eyes. Now makeup
shadows her lids, and she talks
of boys on the phone,
soccer games and pasta parties.

III

No matter that I merely listen.
I am thankful to have them
gathered about me,
thankful to hear their chatter,
feel their warmth as soothing
as the water hushed against
the rocks outside the window.

Swans Flying

They flew close over the water
   for me to hear their whirring,
     more insistent than bows
       across cellos in a sustained refrain,
        more urgent than runners
          in a race, their breathing evenly sure,
           more destined than trains
             clicking fast, steady on their track,
             more eager than my willing
               the strolling light of the long,
             companionable days
                 of spring to come

when illusions of undisturbed calm
   are realized
     at least for awhile.

An Offering

They stand,
three glass vases
in a row
on a black wooden platform
low on the floor--
three glass vases,
tall, medium and small
as an offering
to dull, diminish, and dispel
the prickly spikes of my unease.

Small glass gems
as if placed by themselves
in between the vases
seal the spell of calm
forbidding discontent
or harm to enter.

Coda

"Thy firmness makes my circle just ,
And makes me end, where I [began]."
John Donne

No Need to Wander

It is a fleecy day on a summer street
in a New England town
where couples walk hand in hand
and smile passing by.

In a New England town
we are on our way
while we smile passing by
thinking of the time ahead.

We are on our way
where dusty thoughts will clear
as we think of the time ahead
but instead the past will appear

where dusty thoughts will clear
as show tunes of old
will make the past appear
and I will turn to you

because a show tune of old
"My Darling, My Darling"
will make me turn to you
with the romance of our youth

and "My Darling, My Darling"
washes your face young
with the romance of our youth,
and two young people walk,

their faces washed young
shining along a lengthy shore,
where two young people walk,
the dunes pulling them

shining along a lengthy shore
beyond the curve to explore,
the dunes pulling them.
But the moment of young love

beyond the curve to explore
re-seeds in the dark of the theater
this moment of young love
and there is no need to wander

but recede into the dark of the theater
where couples walk hand in hand
and there is no need to wander
beyond a fleecy day on a summer street.

To order additional copies of *Through the Trees of Autumn* please send your name and mailing address with a check made out to Janet Krauss for $12.00 for each book. Price includes handling, delivery and taxes. Send to:

Janet Krauss
c/o Spartina Press
585 Gilman Street
Bridgeport, CT 06605

Allow two weeks for delivery.

For inquires please send e-mail to bkrauss@snet.net
On Subject line enter Spartina Press.